Inner Circle

Inner Circle

Focus & Fulfillment Habits of the Enlightened

by

Mycal Anders

Inner Circle: Focus & Fulfillment Habits of the Enlightened © 2019 by Mycal Anders.

www.feedmefuelme.com
Anders.Mycal@gmail.com

Print Book ISBN: 978-1-950370-00-9
eBook ISBN: 978-1-942707-99-8
Library of Congress Control Number: 2019932433

Printed in the USA.

 Published by Silver Torch Press.
www.SilverTorchPress.com
Jill@SilverTorchPress.com

Dedication

This book is for Nicole, Trystan, and Camryn.

Your faith has become my courage.

Table of Contents

Foreword

The author is an unappreciative, cheating, dick-of-a-friend, copulating with mentees, broke angel of a human being. Well, at least at one of those he doesn't mention in this book.

If that doesn't sell a book, I don't know what will!

Therein lies why this is such an enlightening read. He's brutally honest of his past mistakes and how they've led to create the man that I know and respect today. Each mistake is a life lesson. This book will give you fuel for conversation and thought around the campfire for months.

Mycal and I met through a sports meetup that I hosted years ago in Phoenix, Arizona. He quickly became a good friend and one of those people where no dream is too big to share. In my line of work, I've become accustomed to meeting hopeless big dreamers. However, what drew me to Mycal was that he is also a big doer. Simply put, he does what he says he'll do. If we're meeting for coffee at 8 am, he'll already have finished his blueberry scone by the time I walk in at 8:10 every single time. It annoys me that he's never late, but yet I respect it deeply. His character has shown in his success in business and in the words of this book. It's no Readers Digest, but Men's Journal picked Mycal's gym as the #1 CrossFit Gym in America in 2017. Do you know how many CrossFit gyms there are in America? Me neither, but there are a lot! I'm putting that in the foreword because Mycal is the type of humble guy that I had to convince to even add that accomplishment to his business website.

So now that I've fluffed his character a little bit (but not too much to where he becomes cocky) here's why Mycal undeservedly asked me to write the foreword. My life's work is helping people build their legacy and finding clarity in what they stand for. I've worked with over 1400 professional athletes to date on that mission through my company, Athletes Brand, and I'm beyond obsessed with the boundaries of the mind's impact on the physical world. (I clearly do not have the same reservations with humility as Mycal.) His teachings in this read are directly in line with what I do, teach, and have studied daily for the past 10 years.

With that, Mycal also knows me well enough to know that I will call B.S. when I see it. It was a bit of a gamble for him to honor me with the task of doing this foreword, I must say. After reading the pages thrice over, and being two months late on the delivery of it, Inner Circle hits home for me. This is a masterful book of success and mindset that should be on every coffee table and given as a gift to your new clients and colleagues. He combines his personal struggles with stories of triumph, along with strategy that you can actually implement. This isn't an autobiography where it's just stories about himself; this is a life guide with relatability and plans of action that had me taking notes the whole way through. He's truly walked the walk, and he shares that journey with the reader.

If you finish reading this book and don't feel rejuvenated, more creative, more aware, more prepared, have a new sense of happiness, or are ready to stand up and yell at your annoying neighbor Brad that mows his lawn at 6:30 am every Sunday that you're ready to build your damn legacy and get the hell out of there today, then I don't know what to tell you. Maybe that's just me and my own run on sentences trying to send the message to Brad any way that I can.

Mycal, I apologize for you allowing me to write the foreword, but thank you for putting this together for us. I can't wait for the readers to get past my nonsense and into the pages of your mastery that will impact a lot of lives.

Kyle Mauch
Founder of Athletes Brand
Portland, Oregon
January 31, 2019

Introduction

"I only got this far because of what I did not know."

- Mycal Anders

Someone told me a long time ago that if I wanted to keep a secret, I should put it in a book. Throughout my life, I have had the good fortune to meet some of the most profound individuals on the planet, most of which probably don't even remember our interaction. I come from a family in which education is everything; however, I am not referring to education in the scholastic sense. No, I am referring to the education of the universe (for you believers out there, insert "Higher Power" here).

My parents saw in me an idealist; a young man who viewed the world through rose colored glasses regardless of circumstance or adversity; a human being who gave humanity the benefit of the doubt. Through that vision, I was introduced to people who spoke a different language. I was privy to recurring conversations where ownership of my journey was paramount and worth protecting at all costs. As I became more and

1

more conscious of these concepts and beliefs, I would find myself oftentimes alone and unable to understand why most people did not think this way.

Why do people go out of their way to make each other miserable? Why do people choose to keep others in their lives who do not positively contribute to theirs? Or, more importantly, do not have room for their positive contributions?

Why are people motivated to simply do just enough, only to blame others when they come up short? Why are people seemingly allergic to accountability and being held to a standard that stretches their comfort zone?

I just never got it.

As my life continued to take shape, I manifested some amazingly beautiful relationships and learned a lot of hard lessons as a result of getting in my own way. As I reflect on it all up to this point, the common denominator in every success or failure has been me.

What a revolutionary concept. In each and every interaction—every exchange of energy—I had a role to play; I was partly responsible. Above and beyond circumstances, choices were made. When I accepted this notion as fact, I became forever empowered; I was now in control. Suddenly, I was able to make decisions very quickly, with great clarity. I was free to feel what I needed to feel as emotions arose, and more important, understand that above all else, happiness is a choice.

Now, before we get too far along, let's answer two big questions. The first is, who is this book *not* for?

This book is not for those who believe they have it all together. This book is not for the people that allow their ego to lead the way and make decisions solely on the premise of keeping that ego intact. This book is not for the people that embrace this school of thought, but only to use it as a tool with which to judge others. If you are not open to scrapping what you thought was working, not open-minded enough to accept that two opposing ideals can indeed be true simultaneously, then this is not the book for you.

The second question should be quite obvious at this point. Who *is* this book for?

This answer is much simpler, as I will explain and provide context later in this passage. If you are in search of something beyond yourself; if you are open to being wrong or the possibility to becoming better as a result of an alternative view or deeper understanding; if you want more for yourself, but don't yet have the awareness to create the tools and relationships that facilitate progress, then this is indeed the book for you.

Why did I write this book? Well, a few years ago my good friend, Jeff, and I started the Feed Me Fuel Me podcast together. You see, as Jeff and I got to know each other, we found ourselves immersed in a conversation that I only had with a select few people in my life. In the aftermath of these discussions, without fail, I found myself enriched, more positive, and more productive. After a while, I found myself going out of my way to surround myself with people that operated on this same frequency, and in some cases, above it (those conversations get really interesting).

There are people walking this earth in such a state of awareness and being that they seem to float through the physical world. You know them. You've seen them. You've either been inspired by their presence, or their energy was so powerful that it made you extremely uncomfortable. How you perceive that energy tends to be a reflection of how you view yourself in the world.

These people have a presence about them. When they walk into a room, the energy changes. This is not exclusive to the loud, the boisterous, the extroverts; no, not at all. As I said before, that energy is indeed a state of being. In the Marine Corps, we called it command presence. There are certain people that affect the climate of a situation simply by the way they stand; the way that they speak; the silent, not-so-obvious confidence that resonates from them.

These are the game changers; the thought leaders; the enlightened. The concepts expanded upon in the following chapters are the practices and philosophies that facilitate the mindset of these incredibly fulfilled individuals.

My intention with this book is to condense hundreds of hours of dialogue into eleven chapters that highlight what it truly means to build a legacy bigger than you. This book will shed light on the deep work required to be fulfilled in this life. I will expand your awareness of happiness by harnessing the hundreds of hours of dialogue we've had with some of the most amazing people in world. You may or may not know some of them; most of them, you probably won't. This was also on purpose.

I didn't want to hang my hat on the daily routines and habits of the rich and famous; rather, I wanted to use the humility of these conversations, of those individuals that are seeking to have a positive impact on the world completely absent of a desire to be famous. Some have even stated that not only was being known for their deeds not on their bucket list, but they would rather it stay that way. A common personality trait that continues to show itself is indeed that of humility.

The people living and teaching these lessons embrace the fact that they didn't arrive at this juncture in their lives on accident; nor did they get there without some assistance from time to time. They find value in surrounding themselves with those who know more, have achieved more, and are simply doing more. Intentionally placing yourself in the company of those that embody the education and experience required for you to become the person you need to be to achieve your goals will only expedite the process.

Welcome to the inner circle. This is not the Illuminati. Nothing I am going to tell you in the pages to come is a secret. I was extremely fortunate to be exposed to this way of thinking fairly early in my life. This mindset has given me the courage to take risks when others played it safe. This lifestyle of abundance allows me the energy and bandwidth to create exposure for those who otherwise would continue to wander the world completely unaware of the fact that they are indeed the one thing stopping themselves from achieving all they want in this life. This is my way of giving back all the lessons and opportunities others thought I was worthy of having.

My wish is that you take what is offered here, apply it in your life, and eventually pay it forward so that someone else may indeed create a life of abundance—attracting the health, wealth, and achievement we are all so worthy of, should we choose to live in our light.

I want to thank you for joining me on this journey. You should know that I am ever appreciative of your willingness to expand your vision and approach these concepts with an open mind so that they might impact you on a deeper level above and beyond simple words on paper.

I wish you nothing but abundance in the hereafter. I appreciate you!

Mycal Anders, MS, CSCS

Chapter One
Goal Setting

"Trajectory, not velocity."

- Aaron Hinde

Life is hard enough as it is. It is even harder when you don't know where you are going. In the conversations I've had over the years with people who live life on a higher level, one of the common denominators is that they are driven by goals.

Not only do they set goals, but they speak those goals to the universe so their inner circle can hold them accountable. That accountability can be deliberate in the form of outsourced coaching and mentorship (more on this later), or intimate like a close friend who simply checks in to see where they are in their process.

Above and beyond simply setting the goal to be held accountable to, putting yourself out there for the world adds an additional element of pressure that drives progress. This is a circumstance in which the ego can work in your favor. The fear of failure or the potential perception of an inability to follow through can be a positive tool.

For these individuals, integrity is priority number one. It is one thing to try and to fail. It is another issue entirely to simply quit because things became challenging or you met unforeseen obstacles.

This book exemplifies this point perfectly. I wrote my first book some years ago, simply as a personal challenge to myself to see if I could do it and whether I would enjoy the process. As a result, I discovered how much I did not know about not only writing, but about the publication process as well. After bloodying my nose a little writing it on my own, I got the book out there. Along the way, I had people asking about it: when it was going to be released, how far along I was, could they get an autographed copy as soon as possible. No pressure, right?! That is exactly my point.

After that experience, I found that I truly loved the writing process, so here I am now; I have a select few individuals who read passages of text as I go. I have a coach I check in with periodically to make sure I am not only writing, but also on track to get this thing published by my intended deadline. I also joined a group of both experienced and novice authors that are somewhere on the way to publishing their own works.

By setting goals that stretch us and demand us to acquire new skills, habits, or disciplines, we are able to have massive objectives come to fruition. A by-product of going through these processes, on top of the gratification of achievement, is the newfound capability to confidently step into a bigger version of yourself. Those skills, habits, and disciplines don't simply disappear once you've conquered a massive task; no, they are with you for the rest of your life; your bandwidth is forever increased, which allows you to operate and take on tasks that demand an increased capacity.

Efficiently attaining these skills to see a goal through to the end is only possible if you have a bit of understanding of what skills or resources you currently lack that inhibit a goal from being realized. This awareness can be brought to light by building a plan, not necessarily in what you should do first, but what you'll need at the end to cross the proverbial finish line.

Setting goals allows you the opportunity to reverse engineer the process, to build the parachute on the way down. In the Marines, we called this mechanism the reverse-planning process. By working backwards from the objective, you can get a real perspective on what is standing between you and massive change. Not having all the answers is a pain in the ass; however, I can tell you from firsthand experience, there is nothing more frustrating than not knowing what questions to ask.

When I opened my first gym, I had no idea about the business end of entrepreneurship; I simply knew the shin-bone was connected to the knee-bone, and I could count to ten really well. When I committed to going brick and mortar—to building my brand—I had to quickly acknowledge how much I did not know, and I started throwing myself at the feet of those within arm's reach who were already doing my deal, and doing it well. I started asking questions.

The answers to those questions led to more questions. For me to sit here and tell you that this part really motivated me to get off my ass and make it happen, I would be lying. In a lot of cases, you find out that what you want to do isn't as simple as you may have originally thought it was. You begin to discover how much money you will have to save or put up or how much time you will have to put in; there are things required that will take the involvement of other people, that what you expected to be done tomorrow won't be completed for another month. This can, without a doubt, be unnerving, overwhelming, and discouraging all at the same damn time.

Here's the good part though: *you're growing*. The breakdowns you have in the middle of the day and the breakthroughs you have at three in the morning are all part of the process. These things occur when you begin to create friction. The best part is that you have chosen these problems. They are not problems that were bestowed upon you by someone else or other external influences; this fact alone makes the process bearable. Because you have made a conscious decision to become a more enlightened, better-equipped version of yourself, you will have the innate persistence to weather the storm that you will inevitably create in your own head. You will take action when everything and everyone around you is telling you to slow down.

You have a goal. You have a plan. You have grown physically, mentally, and spiritually. Because this is a path of your choosing—the inherent adversity that comes along with your choices—you will have the endurance to rise above them. The path to becoming better is never a straight line; however, when you set goals, you have the ability to pivot and adjust course along the way without losing sight of what you originally set out to achieve.

Chapter Two

Have to Start Somewhere

"Your struggle is your story."

- Taylor Dayne Loyd

The journey to accomplish something greater than yourself has to begin somewhere. For most of those in the inner circle, this journey begins subconsciously before their first deliberate steps into the light.

In a later chapter, we'll discuss paying attention to the signs as we move through life. As the universe conspires in our favor, whether it be negatively or positively, that which manifests tends to be what we focus on the most. Those that operate on massive levels often describe the onset of their chosen path as the moment they became conscious of their life's mission or the moment they decided to accept their calling.

As I listened to the description of these amazing individuals' journeys, what became abundantly clear to me was the fact that a critical element of the gift they present to the world is in actuality the result of gifts that were given to them prior to their mission in the here and now. These gifts, be they the overcoming of adversity, meaningful influence in one direction or another, or a set of circumstances requiring them to evolve, come in many forms. It isn't until they stop, take a look back at the occurrences of their lives beyond where they believe to have started, that they realize their entire life up to this point has been grooming them to become who they are.

I became conscious of my journey—my life's purpose—as I spent the better part of two years under the mentorship of one Marc Accetta who made me conscious of entrepreneurship and the value of coaching. From 2006-2007, I attended as many of his seminars as I could possibly afford. At the time, I wanted to hear his message as many times as possible until it became my message. I discovered that the people with the things I wanted and living happily fulfilled lives were always in attendance. I subscribed to the idea that if I attended enough of these seminars and conferences, at some point I would come home with some of the pixie dust that seemed to be filtered through the air vents into the conference rooms. Lo and behold, through this process of immersion, I found myself taking charge of my life, owning my decisions, choosing my circumstances, living life on purpose.

Here's the kicker. Those conferences with Mr. A's (as I would come to address him) mentorship, only brought to the forefront the part of my being that had been drilled into me by my father throughout my entire life. My dad told me long before I encountered Marc Accetta that I should own my own business. He introduced me to the paperwork required to establish a limited liability company, and had me washing cars and selling peaches on the sidewalk to earn money since I was six years old.

As life went on, I found myself recruited by schools for football and track with very little guidance from my parents whose education was paid for by Uncle Sam; paid for in the service as officers in the Air Force. There wasn't a whole lot in the way of financial aid guidance simply because there wasn't a whole lot of experience to draw from. The obvious options for college were either an athletic scholarship or the military. Therefore, I ended up attending the United States Air Force Academy, the best available option.

As I spin the story and connect the dots, however, were I to stay and graduate at the Academy, I would have lost the opportunity to utilize fitness as my platform to effect change and mentor others; not to mention that I was lacking in the departments of life experience and the adversity requisite to learn the lessons of character found in admirable leaders, so the universe conspired in my favor.

I violated the honor code: We will not lie, steal, or cheat, nor tolerate anyone among us who does.

I compromised my integrity by cheating on a test, and because of those choices, I was given the boot. The Air Force Academy sent me packing, hat in hand, silver spoon ripped from my mouth. Now what?

To me, this is where my journey begins, as I moved forward in committing my entire professional and personal education to health and human performance.

What I hadn't accounted for then were the influences of my football coaches, Dominic Zaccarrelli, Kenny Lane, Marlon Curtis; my track coach, Adano Murray; my strength and conditioning coach at Air Force, Allen Hedrick; my parents pushing me to become an Eagle Scout before I got to high school, so nothing would compete with academics and athletics; traveling the world as a military brat, which allowed me to form my own perceptions of how the world really works. All these experiences, circumstances, people, and choices along the way played a role in my journey, which ultimately led to the light I currently stand in.

My entire life has been the accumulation of skills, relationships, and experiences that each had a lesson to teach, which would later be applied in whatever level came next. The journey began long before I knew I was on it. Pay attention.

Chapter Three

Being Anti-Fragile

"Seeking truth instead of trying to be right means that sometimes you are going to be wrong."

- Logan Gelbrich

The enlightened are incredibly protective of their inner circle; who they let in, who they associate with, who they give and seek counsel from, is held in the highest of esteem.

These are the people who prefer to pay full price when someone they know opens a business, rather than seeking a friends-and-family discount. These people have permission to create conflict as a means to sustain accountability. This characteristic rests in reciprocity. These people value each other so much that it is perceived in their best interest to not only call each other on their bullshit, but more importantly maintain a positive relationship in the aftermath.

Those on the inner circle would rather be uncomfortable for five minutes than walk on eggshells and tiptoe around each other until a relationship ultimately withers and dies.

The inner circles of the enlightened welcome the conflict inherent to authenticity and a willingness to be vulnerable. It takes a certain amount of moral courage to tell someone the things he or she does not want to hear; however, if these are to trust in the integrity of each other, a telltale sign of that trust is the results of these conversations.

I beg you not to misinterpret my message. There is not a soul out there who enjoys being wrong; however, when you need to right the ship, make critical adjustments, or simply increase your awareness, it is a huge help to have someone looking from the outside in to point out the things hidden in our blind spots.

This potentially volatile relationship dynamic is welcomed amidst the enlightened. I have even seen when things go unsaid and a project fails or a goal is missed, the person on the receiving end becomes incredibly upset; not because they failed; not because they were hit with unforeseen circumstance; not because they played the role of victim. No. They are upset that another who saw these shortcomings did not take advantage of the opportunity to address them. The opportunity for increased awareness and empowerment to choose whether to keep going or change trajectory was missed. The integrity of the relationship was not upheld.

The mission of the enlightened is to become as anti-fragile as possible. A simple definition—to become stronger as a result of friction. In the context of this book, antifragility means to strategically seek conflict, knowing that you will become better as a result. Physical fitness is an activity that makes the body increasingly anti-fragile. With training that is consistently challenging, the body is able to tolerate more stress in higher doses at increased frequency. The psyches of these people are anti-fragile. Conflict or friction—as challenging or difficult as it may be in the moment—is perceived as a positive experience.

An overlapping theme in my conversations with the enlightened is that there is a lesson to be learned in every experience. The enlightened go out of their way—not to be proven right—but the contrary; they put effort into proving themselves wrong. For the ego-driven individual, this is easily misconstrued as counterproductive. Why would you consciously seek to discover that you are wrong?

Because there is no growth in focusing what is already being done correctly, exceptionally, accurately, or any other adjective that describes precision and efficiency. What you are doing right should be painfully obvious. The improvement comes from acknowledging gaps in systems; the services you do not provide, the tasks that are not being completed, the customers that are dissatisfied, and so on.

While the things we do well should be cultivated and optimized, there is always a place to improve, no matter at what level you're playing. An athlete like LeBron James doesn't spend a ton of time working on his vertical jump. Why? Because he already jumps out of the arena! Instead, he spends time on the less probable elements of his game—shooting midrange and long-range jump shots. If he gets to the rim, the ball is going in, but the further away he gets, the probability of missing increases. In knowing that, it makes sense to increase the probability of success as much as possible by shooting shot after shot, alone and contested, from as many spots on the floor as possible.

In the context of business, when a receptionist is hired to answer the phone, that is definitely a great position to be in. Knowing that you will never miss a prospect or that you now have the ability to address member issues immediately is great; however, the anti-fragile business owner takes it one step further and ensures the phone is not only answered but answered well. He or she will go out of his or her way to create policies in which the phone is answered the same way each and every time; scripts are created, role playing occurs, objections are rebutted over and over again until it becomes engrained in the culture of the business that indeed the phone will be answered this way and customer interaction will occur in this fashion no matter who answers the call.

The enlightened are extremely comfortable being uncomfortable.

My cohost, Jeff, and I almost dropped the Feed Me Fuel Me podcast, but because we have an anti-fragile relationship, we were able to salvage what we've built and ultimately the show. Jeff runs his own company, Land of Lean. I run my own company, CrossFit PHX. We came together to create awareness of this inner circle dialogue. There have been times in which our individual initiatives overlapped, and most of the time, things went off without a hitch. In this particular instance, however, I had just accepted the notion that I do indeed run a business and came full circle with treating it as such. You see, I had a bad habit in my business of letting those close to me off the hook with obscene discounts on memberships, and other endless favors. Through some very anti-fragile coaching, it was brought to my attention how this was hurting my business and inhibiting the attainment of my goals. It just so happens that as I had this revelation, I was not yet versed in the discussion of charging friends and family fairly as I would any other stranger in a business transaction.

Jeff came to me wanting to rent the gym to shoot his products for some promotional material. I had no price set in my head for such a thing, much less for him, a good friend and business partner. The old me would have simply chalked it up as a loss and let him use the space for free; that is not good business, however, so I ignored his correspondence for a few days until I ran into him at the gym. At that point, I gave him a rate as nonchalantly, and admittedly as passive-aggressively as I could, and moved immediately into a conversation with another member. *Total dick move.*

Here's the kicker: Jeff expected me to charge him! There was no expectation of anything free. To make things worse, he wasn't even expecting a discount. The price is the price. His expectation, I would later learn, was to simply get a quote so he could make the best decision with the options he had available. He was looking to me because he would rather enrich my business if it suited the requirements of his mission, rather than outsource it somewhere else.

To this end, we agreed on terms and he did the shoot.

A few days later, Jeff shows up to the gym in regular clothes, no gym bag, and asks if we can talk. I already knew what he wanted. He would express to me that the manner in which I handled this transaction was completely unacceptable. Here is where I'm supposed to become defensive, posture up, and let my ego lead the way. I could have said, "Well you didn't have to take the deal. I assumed you had other options."

But no, I took in everything he had to say. I looked at the sincerity of his body language and proceeded to explain the evolution I was in the process of making and admitted to completely shitting on our relationship. My willingness to be vulnerable and simply admit that I had no idea what I was doing, Jeff's empathy for the process, and our combined priority of open dialogue and pulling no punches for the greater good salvaged our relationship, the show, and our mutual respect for each other.

Since then, Jeff and I are thriving in the podcast space and have had many uncomfortable conversations that put the greater good of each other's goals at the forefront. The friction makes us better, as we are not about being right; we are about living in the truth.

Chapter Four

Self-Identity

"I never identified much as a coach.
That relationship required too much.
I always saw myself as an instructor in terms of my ability to
get information out to those that would then use it in their
teachings."

- Doug Larson

There is so much psychology here that I will keep it anecdotal to keep the narrative interesting and avoid talking over your head while making a complete ass of myself.

I was recently featured in a documentary in which we talked about life after sports and, in my case, the military. Throughout the documentary, there is a common theme that is not exclusive to my journey alone. That theme is transition—leaving the old self behind and embracing the next phase of our evolution. You see, when athletes transition away from sports, or Marines away from active duty, there is a period of adjustment in which we come face to face with competing ideals of how things are versus how they used to be. It is easy to fall into the trap of trying to fit a round peg into a square hole by holding on to the identity of athlete or war-fighter after we have become civilians. Good, bad, or indifferent, the rules of the game have changed, and some assimilation is required to thrive and succeed.

The character traits that I derived from the world of sports and the Marine Corps have definitely helped me to succeed and overcome adversity. No doubt. To maintain that lens as I perceive the world now, however, would only lead to more frustration than fulfillment.

As I transitioned away from sports and later the military, I found myself unappreciative of the skills and tools I had gained from those experiences. My work ethic, decisiveness, fortitude, bravado, candor, tact, and endurance were subverted simply because I was annoyed at the fact that nothing was open at seven a.m., the extreme lack of appreciation for the f-bomb in society, and the work day ending at five p.m. rather than when the job was completed.

Had I chosen to live in that past identity—in an environment that lacked the urgency of mission accomplishment, the directness of objectivity, or the culture of anti-fragility—I would have simply been labeled the *angry veteran* and found myself depressed and alone in a dark room.

All those things made me the obvious choice, however, to accept into grad school, hire on as a new trainer, and ultimately invest in to get my business off the ground by seeking quality mentors and creating an inner circle that helped me reframe all those skills, tools, and character traits that once justified my frustration.

None of the aforementioned opportunities grow legs without a willingness to forego my ego, changing my perspective as my circumstances had changed.

The enlightened have a heightened state of awareness that allows them to be introspective without being too judgmental. This introspection facilitates a process of checking in with oneself. They afford themselves the opportunity to be open and honest with the state of their lives and their subsequent perceptions of it. The inner dialogue changes from one of reaction to the world's impressions upon them to constant seeking of truth, who they need to become, and what tools need be procured to thrive within the world they aspire to create. These honest conversations within give them an opportunity to be honest with themselves and ask deeper questions as to whether or not their course requires rerouting or if they're still participating in the right activities for the right reasons.

Introspection makes them more self-aware, allowing them to pivot or change course as needed without holding it against themselves. Much like the previous chapter, introspection garners a stronger sense of self and purpose that keeps us accountable to ourselves and the task at hand for the greater good. Similarly, it also grants the enlightened the permission to drop dead weight that accumulates in their lives as they take stock in how people and things do or do not serve them in becoming the best version of themselves.

These activities and conversations that go on inside our heads, and sometimes out loud depending on how long the red light might be, build on who we perceive ourselves to be. This, in turn, gives us the freedom to take action in that light through the lens of who we are becoming, not who we are or who we were.

Chapter Five

Application Leads to Mastery

"That book changed the game for me."

- Adee Cazayoux

The thirst for knowledge is real in the enlightened. Those in the inner circle are voracious readers. Over the course of our interviews, there is no shortage of titles to add to an ever-growing list.

As we have these conversations, it seems the inner circle comes with required reading. It never ceases to amaze me as I continue to interact with people on the journey of self-improvement, as well as those that are years ahead of me, a seemingly quick and easy litmus test of your commitment to growth is to purely ask about the books you've read.

The answer to this question almost always proves to validate how deeply you are able to get with a stranger who has yet to be vetted by another member of your inner circle. There is an appreciation for certain titles such as Don Miguel Ruiz' *The Four Agreements*,

Brené Brown's *Daring Greatly*, or Paolo Coelho's *The Alchemist*, to name a few.

Reading books you find in the self-help section of Barnes & Noble or Audible is all well and good, but it means absolutely nothing if you are not willing to apply that information. I have seen it time and time again in coaching and mentorship, when people spend up to thousands of dollars on guidance, only to willingly go against the grain, completely ignoring the advice that they just cut a check to receive. Too often, I have seen people on a quest to obtain information, acquire credentials, and immerse themselves in theory and rhetoric, with no real intention of at least putting it to work in the real world. Knowledge in the absence of application has a tendency to make you a really smart idiot. That is the kind of exposure that will ruin your credibility faster than anything else.

This is one of the defining criteria of the enlightened. They not only thirst for knowledge to be as technically proficient as possible; they also apply that information in the real world for validation, testing and re-testing to see where it fits and how it can or needs to be adapted to fit the circumstances and environment under which it is being applied. This test-retest method is not from an egotistical standpoint where the individual goes out of their way to prove the theory right while trying to prove it wrong. No, the enlightened are genuinely interested in accumulating as wide a skillset as possible while shedding the information that doesn't work or has become outdated by evolution in their field.

In my life, there were endless examples of guidance provided by mentors that was disconfirming to my previously-held belief system. As I have grown and consciously pushed my ego aside, I discovered the very real idea that I am confident these people have my best interest at heart, and until proven otherwise, their wisdom is to be trusted, even if it is uncomfortably foreign to me. Chances are that uncomfortable feeling stems from the requirement to grow and stretch myself beyond my current base of knowledge and skill.

I distinctly recall an instance with a mentee of mine in which I cautioned him about how close he should allow himself to get with his clients; that the proverbial line in the sand should be drawn somewhere before you allow yourself to get carnal knowledge. It's not good business practice to sleep with your clients. Rarely do they ever become your penguin, your lobster, or whatever Discovery Channel euphemism you want to use to describe a monogamous life partner.

Why did I give him this guidance? Because a long time ago, I violated this same principle, hooked up with a couple of my clients, and it exploded in my face, on as public a stage as you could create at closing time during finals week at the campus rec center in college. Remember, kids, the odds that the two girls you didn't think knew about each other, would end up on treadmills, side by side, talking about you while waiting to leave with you, to "relieve the stress of finals week," go up at a small school in east Texas. Just saying.

Anyway, on a mission to prove that he found his unicorn, he took my guidance and threw it out the window. Sure enough, it all came crashing down not long after that. They broke up and he moved on to work somewhere else. This anecdote exemplifies the consequence of the ego leading the way.

Reading the books, attending the seminars, coffee with mentors; none of that matters if you are not willing to apply that information and do not have an inherent trust in those that are providing the guidance. Healthy skepticism is a good thing, however, but not at the expense of your personal growth and development.

Chapter Six

Happiness is a Choice

"Self-care isn't selfish."

- David Lovell

One of the biggest awakenings in the inner circle is the realization of how much control you actually have over your universe. Remember when I mentioned that the enlightened choose their associations with extreme prejudice? You dictate who comes in and out of your life and the roles they play within in it. This is one of the most powerful gifts we have as human beings. With the mastery of our universe comes the reality of choice over circumstance. So much of what happens to you happens because of you and only when you transcend your ego are you able to take responsibility for the role you play in your life. To that end, happiness is indeed a choice.

This is not a simple, idealist, glass-half-full optimist perspective. Not at all. There is solace to be found in knowing that you can indeed choose to be happy, despite your current circumstance. During the best of times, this seems to be irrelevant; during the worst of times, this is a critical choice. The option of happiness dictates so much with regards to how long life's shit storms tend to last. Before I continue, I want to be very clear; you are entitled to feel whatever you need to feel from one moment to the next. People die. Jobs are lost. Fender benders occur. People get trolled on social media. No one is immune to the instances of life; however, your perception of life's doldrums and how long you live in that space is completely up to you. My guidance, as I have practiced and observed in the enlightened, is to feel what needs to be felt, but eventually to come back to happy.

Now that we've established that shit happens to the enlightened, just like it does to everyone else, let's talk about this happiness-choice thing. This thought evolution of choosing happiness provides the endurance to work through adversity. The happiness choice puts you in a productive mindset in which you are able to better problem solve and find a solution to a present dilemma. By choosing to be positive, you grant yourself permission to grow from life's experiences. You are present and open so that the lessons to be learned become obvious, as if you have a highlighter to emphasize the main points in the chapters of your life.

Absent this choice, you only handicap yourself; you are unable to clearly see, much less accept the truth of what happens to you because of you. The fog of friction created by a negative state of mind only places more obstacles in your path that tend to manifest in indecision, procrastination, distraction, depression, and blame. In choosing anything other than happiness, you have chosen to leave center; to leave balance. You have made a decision to live in a state where progress cannot be attained. In this negative state resulting from the perception of negative circumstances, you have given your power away, running away from your inherent strengths in a moment of weakness; a moment of weakness that lasted a few moments too long.

This practice of choosing positive is just that—practice. No one is perfect. Not everything goes as planned. Sometimes we are just blindsided by the unforeseen and crazy.

As I reflect on this concept, there was a period of my life in the immediate aftermath of my father's death where I had to make some very difficult decisions. My father, who was hands-down the most influential person in my life, passed away in his sleep during one of the most transitional periods of my existence. I was home for the holidays prior to entering Marine Corps Officer Candidate School. After he died, there was a period of a couple weeks in which I would listen to my mother cry her eyes out, as she had just lost her best friend, confidant, and life partner. I closed off and locked up. I offered to drop my seat at OCS to stay home and be with her during the challenging time it was for both of us. My mother told me to go forward. She gave me permission to live my life. She assured me that we would all make it through this and that the last thing my father would have wanted was for me to not live my best life due to his passing.

You see, my mother is in my inner circle. She has lived an amazing life; held down a fruitful military career; raised four boys and explored the planet with us and on her own, leaving no stone unturned. In that, she could see what I could not; she knew my best years were ahead of me.

Aside from her, there was nothing for me in Nashville, Tennessee. For me to stay, I would not become who I am as a man, a husband, a father, and an entrepreneur. If I stay, this book doesn't get written. She exposed me to my blind spots. Amidst her own pain and loss, she was able to suspend it all and choose happy while being present and aware. How easy and understandable would it have been to ask me to stay? You see, in choosing happy, she was still able to be selfless and acknowledge the greater good in asking me to go, and see the Marine Corps all the way. Were she to succumb to the tragedy of circumstance surrounding the loss of my father, no one would blame her for being selfish, seeking the perceived comfort of keeping me— or any of us boys, for that matter—home. That is what makes the trait of choice that much more powerful.

This story is just one of many instances in life in which no one would find fault with taking the easy way out. From the outside looking in, making the comfortable decision is justified. People understand why you threw your hands up and let it all fall apart. No one would blame you for any of that; you get a pass.

This fact makes these choices even harder, especially in the beginning of this conscious paradigm shift; however, in choosing happy, progress, and positive— challenging as it may be—you grant yourself the foresight of the greater good, transcending the most trying times to make the best decision for yourself and others in the wakes of those decisions.

Chapter Seven

Getting Over Yourself

"Are you willing to leave life's dumpster behind?"

- Tony Grebmeier

We all have baggage. The enlightened and their respective inner circles came to be because of their baggage. It is part of the journey. Those experiences, those people, those occurrences are supremely influential in framing the lens through which we perceive the world; however, as they say, there is no need to take it with you.

I was taken through an exercise in an interview in which I recounted as many influential events and people in my life as possible. As I went along, naming names and telling stories, they simply piled up in this metaphorical dumpster in front of me.

After a while, we shifted gears, and I was asked about my goals and what I wanted out of life. Those things were ahead of me, on the other side of the dumpster. The only way to get to them was to do what most of us do at first glance and just push that heavy-ass dumpster, full of life's ups and downs, achievements and disappointments, successes and failures. The proverbial dumpster gets heavier and heavier as life goes on. Then I was instructed to simply stop pushing, step back, take a breath and look at the bigger picture.

I was then asked, "What if you just walked around the dumpster and caught up to your goals?" You would have the weight off your shoulders, the obligation of the past erased, nothing but freedom to choose your path lies ahead; seems to be the simplest idea in the world. And it is. Let's not confuse simple with easy though. That would be extremely naïve.

What stunts the growth and overall progress of the unaware— the unenlightened, those without a strong inner circle—towards fulfillment is ego tripping. We allow our ego to do the walking and talking on our behalf, and lose a lot of time, to our detriment.

How often to do we catch ourselves standing in the shadows of who we used to be, as opposed to the light of who we are becoming? How often do we hold our old selves against who we are in the here and now?

No matter how much you have crushed it in life, or many times you have completely shit the bed, all of that is part of your past. There are lessons learned on either side of that coin, in both success and failure, yet there is absolutely no need to stand behind that dumpster and push it along. Another analogy commonly used is the back pack full of rocks in which every stone in that back pack weighs you down and slows your progress. When you begin to unpack those stones and lighten the load, the path becomes much easier and clearer.

One of the biggest catch-22s about life amongst the enlightened is that you have to go through these trials and tribulations and accumulate these experiences to appreciate who you've become and to stand in your light. Your life prior to the present provides context and offers basis for who you are. To stand in your light and be present along the way, it is important to take what is needed from each of those people and experiences, learn the lessons, and then drop that baggage and ego as you continue to move forward.

Put simply, in order to live a fulfilled and abundant life requires the constant getting over of oneself. It is requisite self-work to invest the time for introspection as well as retrospection, to assess your values and belief systems as you evolve as a human being. Who you are is not the same as who you were; on the contrary, who you were only plays a small role in who you are.

As you move through life from one chapter to the next, taking stock of those past experiences will facilitate choices and relationships made in the present that will shape the growth required for the future.

For context, I learned the lesson of integrity in the wake of getting kicked out of the Air Force Academy. I learned the lesson of selflessness from my mother after my father passed away. I learned how to apply leadership and decision making as a Marine where the mission had priority over convenience. I learned from my mentors that sacrifice is required to accomplish anything great; these were mentors who had been in my shoes as I was building the gym, sleeping in the gym, mopping the floors, coaching the classes, and selling the memberships while finishing grad school.

These events, people, and lessons were required for me to become who I am; however, I do not hang on those things and hold them against myself today. I have grown as a result of those occasions. How I lead, the importance of integrity, and service before self are all part of who I am as a result of my past lives. They have forged the lens with which I see the world and assess my inner circle.

In order to move into the next chapter of your life, take the lessons, not the baggage. Who you were is not who you are. You will be obligated to get over yourself in order to get out of your own way and play at the next level.

Chapter Eight

Mentorship

"I don't care if you know the answer. What I care about is if you know where to find the answer when you need it."

- Captain Michael "Mia" Hyde, USMC

My favorite leaders in the Marine Corps were the ones that promoted small unit leadership above micromanagement. My platoon commander, Captain Michael Hyde at The Basic School always emphasized that as most important. He introduced me to a hierarchy of organizational leadership that I impart daily: Mission, Marines, Me.

When the mission takes precedent, all decisions are made with the greater good in mind, regardless how uncomfortable it makes the team. If you need justification for kicking in this door, taking that hill, or picking up this piece of trash, you need look no further than the mission. In order to succeed, these are the things that must be done. In business, the vision or key performance indicators (which we'll get into later), when explained adequately, are the purpose for doing anything. The mission is your why.

This simple word at the top of the hierarchy makes things incredibly easy to understand, in turn making compliance to orders greater. When your subordinates, coworkers, or peers do not understand why certain duties must be undertaken, then they do not fully understand the mission. In Marine-speak, the commander's intent. If you, as a leader have trouble pulling the proverbial trigger on a controversial yet necessary decision, then you have failed to come back to the mission. In my experience as a Marine, not only did the best leaders eat last, they also led with why and purpose.

My commanding officer, Lieutenant Colonel John Barranco, while we were deployed to Afghanistan, sent me with a contingent of Marines and civilian contractors to an outpost, Forward Operating Base (FOB) Edinburgh, to extend our range for intelligence, surveillance, and reconnaissance. I had no idea what I was doing, let alone what was needed to set up an outpost to enhance combat operations during one of the most kinetic periods of Operation Enduring Freedom. These are not the things they teach you at Marine Operational Specialty (MOS) School, for which I was an air traffic control officer. All I could come back to was the mission and my Marines. Everything else would fall into place. By placing priority on the first two elements of the hierarchy, I had faith I would be taken care of.

We departed for the unknown of the Sangin Province, Afghanistan. I leaned heavily on my Marines to be the incredible subject matter experts they were. As a young, dumb Lieutenant, I remember the guidance given to me by my mother, father, godfather, and every other officer that made it past company grade, and that was to lean heavily on your staff non-commissioned officers until you have your feet under you, and also to trust my training and my Marines' training to accomplish the mission. Young officers in these scenarios are notorious for allowing their ego to lead the way. They are so hung up on being in charge that they can fail to lead. It was imperative that I trust my Marines to be phenomenal professionals until proven otherwise. They never let me down.

In doing so, we successfully built an outpost in the middle of nowhere so that we were able to keep an eye on our fellow Marines on the ground as they got down and dirty with enemy combatants. My Marines deserve all the credit for the success of our operation. I simply listened to their guidance and made sure they were able to do their jobs uninhibited by the flagpole or other agencies on that outpost with us. By turning them loose to think outside the box and do more with less, my

Marines then took ownership of our mission and made it their own.

Much of my leadership style as a Marine, and now as an entrepreneur, comes from the guidance I got from quality mentors and leaders throughout my time in training. When shit got real and decisions had to be made to stay on station longer with low fuel, to keep Marines on shift a little longer in support of a chaotic engagement with the enemy, foregoing my coveted Chili-Mac MRE so one of my Marines could have the cornbread inside, I only had to come back to three words that made the hard decisions just a little bit easier: Mission, Marines, Me.

This is the guidance that I have not found to be readily available in the civilian world. As I spend more time amongst the enlightened, I have found that they are active seekers of mentors and leaders; each with a specific purpose, most with a finite period of service. What is understood amongst those in the inner circle is that there are subject matter experts and mentors for literally everything. There are people out there that consult on matters that take your company from $100,000 gross per year, to $100,000,000 gross. There are coaches out there that will expose the inability, or inaccuracy of communication with your significant other, to enhance your rocky relationship. There are mentors that will challenge you to make hard decisions that you would not make otherwise. Each and every one of them serves a purpose and exists to equip you with the tools, knowledge, and accountability to play your game at a higher level, whether that is business, relationships, or life.

This supporting cast of professionals derives its reputation from the success that it has helped others achieve, far beyond any of the success that it has seen personally. This is indeed one of the telltale signs of seasoned coaches or mentors: whose story are they telling? Theirs or their clients'?

In the final conversation with my previous coach whom I hired to help me with financial clarity in my business, after having me take a good, hard look at my business and the infamous numbers I was so afraid of, he left me with this:

"Alright, this is the end of the road. You now know everything you need to know to accomplish the goals that we set out for. Everything after this is your fault."

I cannot thank him enough. There isn't a price high enough for peace of mind. Quality mentorship isn't hard to find. You must be aware enough to seek it out and recognize it when you see it. Be humble enough to stand on the shoulders of giants as you grow into their shoes and begin walking on your own.

Lastly, as the enlightened move from one level to the next in whatever phase of life it is, they reach down and pull others up behind them, finding opportunities to be the mentors they once required for another.

Chapter Nine

Legacy

"My crowning achievement? That's the easiest one of all: my kids."

- Coach Mike Burgenor

You can manifest all the money in the world. You have the tools to accumulate all the toys an adult child could ever want. You can travel the world and see all that can be seen; however, as I walk with the enlightened, they all realize that they cannot take any of that with them in the great hereafter.

Why the hell are we doing all this?

What's it all for?

What makes it worth it?

The easy thing to do would be to absolve yourself of struggle altogether. Go through the motions. Do all the things you are supposed to do; nothing more, nothing less. Live a life absent of impact, serving only yourself, being comfortable on autopilot.

That doesn't sound very exciting, does it?

Here is the reality of the situation. Impact is relative. On the planet earth, there is a theory out there that is embraced in the inner circle, that people are doing the best they can with the tools they've been given. The fourth agreement of Paulo Cohelo's book is to "always do your best". Your best is a sliding scale.

As you level up and your awareness increases, so does your relative best. As we become enlightened, our circle of influence grows and with it our ability to cast a wider net. However, impact seems to have rings like that of the ripples in a pond after a pebble has been dropped.

The inner circle drives impact and creates legacy from the inside out. Much in line with self-care not being selfish, it all starts within; with the person staring back at you in the mirror. You have to face yourself every day and determine whether or not you are living your truth, or someone else's. When you are walking in your light with intention, you now have energy in abundance. In this state of flow, you are the example others will look to for influence, motivation, and inspiration.

On my path to writing this book, I have found that much of my journey was based on the practice of what felt right and what felt good. When I wake up every morning before the sun cracks the horizon knowing that I am living my purpose, on purpose, it is invigorating. The energy I have day to day is replenished by the feedback I get from others in the form of a smile or hearing what struck them about this week's episode of Feed Me Fuel Me. It literally lights my fire knowing that the happiness my children see in me is reflected in their happiness. My fulfillment in life bleeds over into my marriage, ensuring that the first words out of my mouth each and every day are, "I love you," to my wife.

It is important that we start with, "Why?". There is no mission absent of purpose. As I was pushed through an exercise with a coach some years back, I made a very insightful, albeit painful, discovery. On the surface, I started my gym to get people in the best shape of their lives. I felt I could do it better than anyone else in the game. I never wanted to wear a uniform or suit and tie to work ever again.

But in this exercise, that I affectionately call the "7 Why's", I was getting pushed deeper and deeper; uncovering layer after layer. After I gave an answer, I was immediately met with another "Why", ultimately uncovering that the commitment to my life's work in fitness spawned from watching my father make horrible health decisions: inactivity, smoking, soda, fast food, etc. All of this ultimately led to his passing, much earlier than I feel he should have.

In this moment, I uncovered a promise I had made to myself in my teens. If I didn't have the power to change my dad, then I'd be damned if I didn't try to change everyone else for the better. And there it is: my truth.

All other endeavors that didn't culminate in helping people achieve a healthier, happier life were for naught. Any attempts to do something else had luke-warm enthusiasm at best and fizzled out quickly.

The things that grew and became wildly successful—my gym, my podcast, my books—were in line with my truth, my vision, and my legacy.

You see, when it is all said and done, it is not about impacting the world. What a lofty goal, an admirable one at that. Yet, you must be an inspiration to yourself first. Whether it is conscious or subconscious, people will recognize this and respond to you in kind. Even then, as your influence and impact grow, and your ripples have now become wakes, it is still only possible to impact a single person at a time. Where it gets really interesting is when your impact is reciprocated and those you've empowered are now taking responsibility for their own happiness, and in turn empowering others to do the same.

Now your wake has become a wave. Indirectly, you now have created a legacy. Your cup runneth over, as they say. Now you're writing books, sharing stories, dropping podcasts, blogging, having meetings that spark incredible ideas! Impacting the masses, one reader, one listener, one viewer, one client at a time. All of this comes to fruition because you answered one simple question in the affirmative: "Am I living my truth?"

Answering yes to this one question empowers you to be a person of impact. Creating a legacy that will live on past you. Leaving the world a better place than it was when you found it.

Chapter Ten

Pay Attention to the Signs

*"It's not that you haven't heard it or seen it before.
The fact of the matter is, you see what you need to see, read
what you need to read, hear what you need to hear, when you
need it most."*

- Mike Arce

In the game of introspection that is played amongst those in the inner circle, a theme of pattern recognition manifests. As they look back and analyze events that have taken place or habit patterns responsible for the present, the deeper they go, certain outcomes and similar instances are often repeated.

I have experienced this phenomenon over and over in my quest of self-improvement. Through the guidance of my coaches, I have come to accept as fact that habits are not broken, they are replaced. There are things I do that increase my productivity, and others that halt me in my tracks.

Over the years, I noticed that when I needed to make a massive decision that instilled an element of fear, I would get a sickening feeling in my stomach, as if my guts were realigning on their own. For me, ironically, this feeling also arises when I skydive out of an airplane. How funny is it that the feeling of fear and excitement physically manifest the same way?

What this feeling represents is circumstantial and left to perception. It can push you over the edge or be debilitatingly paralyzing. When faced with this gut feeling, using information from previous experience has been required for me to analyze the purpose of this momentary, gut-wrenching paralysis. Am I scared or am I excited? You would think those two extremes are nothing alike, and yet, they are more alike than you might think at face value.

I will never forget the excitement I once felt at my first football practice. With regards to my brothers, I was late to the game. My big brother, our family's warchild, thrived in the spaces where his medal was tested. He would grow up to become an infantry Marine and volunteer for a second deployment to Iraq during Operation Iraqi Freedom after experiencing the Spartan lifestyle of a wartime Marine. My little brother, our family's champion, competed simply to discover how good he truly was. He had a lot of natural size, speed, strength, and talent. He has been on a journey to harness that raw athleticism, combined with hard work to see where his physical potential truly lies. In college, he would win a national title, go on to try out with a few professional teams, and is now climbing the ladder in the Ultimate Fighting Championship. Watching them strap on their pads and come home bragging about the hits they doled out or who they juked out of their shoes was always intriguing to me, but where my big brother was crazy, and my little brother was a freak, I was in the middle, thinking way too much and having to work real hard.

My first practice was interesting to say the least. I don't remember splitting up into the positions that we thought we should play. No. We put our mouthpieces in and circled up. One player at a time was called in the middle of the circle and coach said, "Get 'em hot!". Upon command, there were 40 or so kids chopping our feet, running in place. It was in the best interest of the poor bastard in the middle to keep his head on a swivel. We kicked off our first full pad practice with a period of "bull in the ring". As our pads are clicking, our toes are popping, and coach screams out the number of a player in the mob. If that number is yours, you fly in and do your best to de-cleat the guy in the middle. The "bull" is simply required to stand his ground, absorb the blow, and keep chopping his feet in anticipation of where the next hit is coming from.

As you figure out very quickly, you have nothing to lose if you're on the perimeter awaiting your number to be called so you can hopefully catch the bull off guard and lay him on his back. As the drill continues, and the yells and chants grow louder, it is sensory overload.

Now, it's my turn. I'm the bull. My pads are warm from running in and trading licks with the handful of bulls before me. I thought I was ready. "27!" Smash. "19!" Crunch. "83!" Boom. "53!" Pop. I am holding my ground, giving as much as I am getting, and still standing. Then it all changed.

"32!"…

The next thing I know, I am flat on my ass, gasping for air. Coach called the number of the guy directly behind me at my 6 o'clock. Before I could turn around, his facemask was in my earhole, and my feet were no longer attached to terra firma. What happened next was the biggest surprise and would be my first recollection of the simultaneous conundrum, "Am I scared or excited?"

"Get up, you're still going," my coach exclaimed. Without a lot of time to think about it, my instincts took over and my arousal peaked instantly. I was excited! Let's do it. "68!" Bang!

That experience led me on a path that would eventually pay for college and instill in me leadership qualities I would hone and employ as an officer of Marines.

This feeling showed up when I stood at the thick red line at the entrance to Officer Candidate School. It was present when I was presented the opportunity to go brick and mortar with CrossFit PHX. It was there when I jumped out of a plane for the first time. It was there when I was given command of my detachment of Marines in Afghanistan and given a mission I did not feel qualified to accomplish. That constriction of my bowels showed up on the first kick off of every game I ever played.

As I sit back, periodically faced with these various decision points in my life, I discovered that this feeling is indeed a sign. It is an indicator of a risk about to be taken. On the other side of that risk is massive reward. That reward has shown up as money, recognition, personal growth, opportunity, or any combination of the above. In knowing that, I choose to be excited and push forward, often times into the unknown, rather than be paralyzed by the fear of what may, or may not come to reality.

Pay attention to the recurring signs in your life. What often shows up as fear for the unaware tends to manifest as excitement for the enlightened.

Another recurring theme in these discussions with people living on a higher frequency is what people say about them, to them. When it comes to starting your own business or moving away from your current employer, first and foremost it should be in line with your plan and purpose. I will lead with this disclaimer: if you do not desire to take the risks associated with going out 100% on your own, nothing anyone will tell you is going to change that, so don't.

As we've taken the deep dive into discussing some of the catalysts for massive change for the enlightened, there is reinforcement that takes place from external sources. The first is the recurring idea that whatever you are doing for someone else can be done better, or that you would simply do it differently. The second is the reinforcement of the idea that is demonstrated in other's concurrence that you should indeed strike out on your own.

I had people tell me I should open my own facility for nearly a decade before I actually did it. All the while, I showed up at the gym every day—whether it was Gold's Gym in my early twenties, leading physical training in the Marine Corps, or the country club I trained in while at grad school—and say to myself, "There is no way I should be placed in the same category as these other guys. If I had my own place, I would make sure the quality of trainer was impeccable, and things would be done differently."

One day, opportunity struck. A client of mine asked me if I had ever wanted to start my own place. "Of course," I replied.

She asked how much it would cost and offered to back me. I would be lying if I told you I was completely prepared for this conversation. Truth be told, I was smiling to her face but in my mind, I was shitting my pants. I ran the idea by another client of mine that had become a mentor and friend. His response was, "When was the last time someone offered to make your dream come true?"

"Never."

"When do you think it will happen again?"

"I don't know."

"You have a lot going on with grad school and all; however, the wonderful thing about human beings is our ability to figure shit out."

"I hear you."

"Let me be more direct. Figure it the fuck out!"

And so I did. Nothing becomes more obvious than watching the universe align in your favor and the proverbial signs I've been referencing in this chapter go from the mundane exit-here kind to the bright lights of fucking Vegas. I did the deal. I figured it out. Five years later my gym, CrossFit PHX, was rated the number-one CrossFit box in America!

Not all signs are quite this obvious. Truthfully, more often than not, they aren't. It is in your best interest to be aware. Take note of the recurring themes in your life and live in the flow of opportunities as they actualize in your favor.

Chapter Eleven

The Abundance Mindset

"We are in the game of relationships."

- Chris Powell

One of the fundamental laws of the universe is that of reciprocity. When we live in a state of abundance, not only are we in a giving state of mind, but we have also given ourselves permission to receive. The former, as I've discussed with those in the inner circle, can be quite obvious. They recognize that many of their opportunities are either not of their own making or manifest in a collaborative effort with others. Therefore, connecting the dots in recognition of the importance of paying it forward is not a monumental leap. Doing for others as has been done for you in mentorship, time, opportunity, or simple counsel just makes sense.

The latter can be quite difficult for people to grasp, however, yet this is where the abundance mentality comes full circle, no pun intended. For those striving for more, who have begun to look inward and work on self, a catch-22 can occur: how can I be of service to others if I am not yet walking a perfect path?

When living in abundance, giving and receiving operate in harmony; in a state of flow. While you are working on yourself, slowly achieving higher frequencies of thinking, you can begin to push the lessons you've learned against those that are operating at lower frequencies. Those that demonstrate a propensity for action on the lessons you impart are the people you then invest your time and energy into more regularly.

Many get concerned that they will be judged harshly when they begin this journey of self-improvement. There is a preconceived notion that if I share myself with the world, my ideas will be stolen or I will be seen as lesser-than for displaying vulnerability. None of this could be further from the truth.

The intangible that you bring to the table is, quite frankly, *you*. This is the very reason that McDonald's and Burger King exist together, often times on the same block. Yes, they both sell hamburgers, but they offer slightly different experiences and flavor profiles. I use this simple example to make a point. No one will be able to duplicate you or what you specifically bring to the table. It is the nuances of you that cannot be readily duplicated.

Your ability to express vulnerability is not the same as throwing yourself a pity party and expecting everyone to tell you, "It's going to be ok." Quite the contrary. The expression of vulnerability is being humble enough to seek answers when you have questions. It is having the integrity to admit when you messed up or did someone wrong, and making a deliberate attempt to make amends. Vulnerability is acknowledging the fact that you are imperfect, will always have work to do, and continue to recognize lessons in the aftermath of mistakes.

In expressing your vulnerability and sharing yourself with the world, you become open to receive what the universe has to offer. You have given the universe an opportunity to conspire in your favor. By actively seeking not only opportunities to give but also to receive, you are playing an active role in the creation of a state of flow. You will know when you are there because things that were once challenging require less effort. The stuff, money, opportunities; the physical manifestation of progress will come into your life without struggle. Also, the things in your life that are hindering your progress fall by the wayside when you are living in a state of flow and abundance.

Flow occurs in business when you have all the right people playing the right roles and the systems in place to support those efforts—a huge lesson I learned the hard way in the development of my brick and mortar operation. I had spent the first few years operating in a space of scarcity. I wanted to wear all the hats and delegated ancillary responsibilities to my coaches with the expectation that they should also handle memberships and sales. Through this model of mismanaged delegation, we continued to grow, but the grind was real. Everything felt as if it required monumental effort to the detriment of the quality of coaching my staff was able to put forth.

Through the counsel of my coach, he helped me acknowledge the obvious—do less! *What?!* Do less? *How does that make sense?* Here's how. He showed me what proper delegation actually looked like. I hired a front desk person to manage the new member management, sales, and gym tours. In doing so, my coaches were now free to do what they do best—coach classes and train private clients. With this new distribution of effort, we were now in a state of operational flow. Not only were we making more money, a key indicator that the business is doing something right, the morale of my coaches was at an all-time high. We were able to deliver higher quality coaching without distraction, while sales and membership increased because we now had a person whose sole responsibility was simply that.

When you're able to accomplish more with less effort—when you can give more while simultaneously receiving more—that is what flow looks like. You are now in a place where you can operate with clarity and foresight. It takes an abundance mentality to establish flow. Sans an abundance mindset, you will more than likely experience flashes of flow but have no means to sustain it or recreate it.

In life above and beyond business, abundance manifests in fulfillment and having quality relationships. The abundance mindset stimulates enlightenment that isn't forced. You will start attracting into your life growth opportunities and people who seek to grow as you grow. Mentors will begin to take you under their wings when they otherwise wouldn't bother.

As you adopt this mentality, you will, over time, witness your circle change for the better. Those that once took up your time in the existence of the victim will distance themselves, as your actions will demonstrate that the choice to live in that reality is counterproductive. Those spots on your team will be filled with people who realize the single most common denominator in life is self. These people make deliberate efforts to look within first and will hold you accountable to do the same.

The examples you seek to emulate will change as well. What you do not know will frighten you less and less. You will become more adept at requesting assistance and admitting what you do not know—for some, the ultimate exposure of vulnerability. In the ways of the universe, as you seek quality examples to emulate and become, so too will you become the quality example that others will aspire to be.

As you evolve and continue to bet on yourself, the odds will begin to stack in your favor. You will find others who also decide to bet on you, invest in you as a person, and promote your initiatives. All this receiving is a by-product of your newfound mentality only enhances your ability to reciprocate and give back, impart lessons learned, share resources, and ignite ideas in others to be acted upon, as opposed to just consider.

When living in abundance, your intentions are obvious. Your priority is the greater good and witnessing those in your circle experience their best selves. The abundance mentality ignites a state of flow that allows your best self to shine through as you step into your light. The universe will acknowledge your actions and reciprocate accordingly!

Epilogue

"What lies beyond the pale isn't always safe and secure."

- Steven Kotler & Jamie Wheal, Stealing Fire

You will come to find in the adoption of these habits of the inner circle that it is a rather uncommon way of thinking in today's society. So much of today's validation of self is reliant upon external sources that a huge proportion of society has left themselves behind. You hear it in everyday conversation. People describe the events of their lives as if they have no control. The happenings of their existence inevitably happen for a million reasons that are not because of them. These events happen *to* them, not *because of* them. The responsibility for their piece of the equation is watered down to the point of disappearance, diluted in blame and circumstances outside their control.

Every once in a while, you happen upon a person or a group of people who are speaking a different language; a group of people who approach life with a level of introspection that doesn't exist in daily interaction with the human race. Before wallowing in the self-pity typically associated with adverse circumstances, these look inside for a solution to their dilemma, making the quickest work of negative emotion possible so they can move on and move forward in as positive a state of productivity as possible.

You are now privy to how this sect of society speaks, thinks, and acts. Your awareness has now been increased. Should you choose to put these principles into action, you will find your life changed forever; your network, your net worth, your state of being—all changed for the better, forever.

You will no longer let yourself off the hook, nor will you accept mediocrity in your endeavors. You will find yourself in the company of people who will not tolerate those things from you, as they do not accept these shortcomings in themselves.

It is work. It starts with you.

It requires accountability.

This mindset mandates change.

Don't make the mistake that many who begin this transitional period in their lives make and peak at the mountain's precipice. Take it one step at a time and you will eventually crest the summit of enlightenment, operating at a higher frequency; accomplishing more with less effort.

The reality is that your output has a direct correlation with your input. You will put your energy at the top of your priority list. You will find yourself extremely protective of who and what you devote your attention and energy to.

You will seek out new challenges and look forward to the friction in life that stimulates growth. Your perception of life's friction will also change from one of negativity and struggle to the understanding that this is what is actually required if you truly intend to become something great. You will no longer avoid conflict. You will seek out healthy means to force improvement, ever adding to your toolbox, equipping you to handle the challenges yet to come as you continue to grow, and continually living life at a higher level of knowing.

Before too long, you will pick your head up, take a look around, and realize the landscape of your world is drastically different than it used to be when your journey began. The people in your sphere of influence will be different or completely new as a result of your personal evolution.

You will wake up every day with initiative and a smile on your face, ready to attack the day. You'll have a sustainable energy no cup of coffee or energy drink can replicate. You will have changed your mind, and in doing so, changed your life.

For you, I wish all these things and more. My hope is that you apply the principles outlined in this book directly in your life so that you experience a level of fulfillment and happiness that eclipses that which I have had the joy of experiencing.

Thank you for picking up this book. I appreciate the journey you are undertaking and offer nothing but love and support as you create the best version of your life.

It is with the utmost love and support that I write this book. You have your best days ahead of you.

I appreciate you!

Mycal Anders, MS, CSCS

About the Author

Mycal Anders has chosen fitness as his platform for life changes, and he has been blessed to help thousands of people over the past 16 years to not only accomplish their physical and aesthetic goals, but also to overcome life challenges and change their own circumstances.

Mycal learned early that it is important to serve as your own primary source of motivation. Everything that comes thereafter is a bonus. Mycal is here to help empower and educate people to get out of their own way and become the happiest, most productive version of themselves possible.

Using consistent manifestation and affirmation, in combination with a healthy lifestyle, the world is your oyster! Mycal shares with people his story with the intention of making them aware that they are not alone in their journey. Many have walked those footsteps before you, and there will be many after you. Through his experience and the lessons he learned along the way, it is his hope that you are inspired to ignore the naysayers and go after the things in life that you truly want.

- Husband to Nicole - Father to Trystan & Camryn
- USMC Veteran, Operation Enduring Freedom
- Founder of CrossFit PHX, rated #1 CrossFit Box in America 2017
- Cohost, Feed Me Fuel Me Podcast
- Author and entrepreneur with a Masters from Arizona State University

Made in USA - North Chelmsford, MA
1306447_9781950370009
02.23.2022 1623